Danish Cross-Stitch
Zodiac Samplers

Charted Designs for the Astrological Year

Jana Hauschild

Dover Publications, Inc.
New York

Published in Canada by General Publishing Company, Ltd., 30 Lesmill Road, Don Mills, Toronto, Ontario.

Danish Cross-Stitch Zodiac Samplers: Charted Designs for the Astrological Year is a new work, first published by Dover Publications, Inc., in 1980.

International Standard Book Number: 0-486-24032-0
Library of Congress Catalog Card Number: 80-67098

Manufactured in the United States of America
Dover Publications, Inc.
180 Varick Street
New York, N.Y. 10014

Publisher's Note

The sampler has been a popular needlework form for many years in many different cultures. Originally the sampler was actually a "sampler" or "exemplar" of stitches, attesting to the ability of its maker, usually a young girl. The completed sampler was a needlework lesson as well as a reference chart of stitches. Often the alphabet, in various styles, was the start of the stitchery lesson, and after that technique was accomplished, the remainder of the block could be embellished to show the other accomplishments of the embroiderer. Decorative borders and figures, such as houses, pets, mottoes and other objects close to the heart of the embroiderer, were introduced. Many examples of these early lessons on linen have been preserved in homes and museums.

Today the sampler is no longer merely a diploma to be displayed by a proud parent, but has become a decoration for the home. Today's sampler displays not only the expert technique of the stitcher, but often reflects the interests and imagination of the maker. A modern sampler can portray family interests, hobbies, travels and occupations.

The samplers in this book—all of which appear in full color on the covers—have been designed by Jana Hauschild, one of the most creative designers working in Denmark today. They are based upon the twelve signs of the zodiac, one sampler for each sign of the year. Following tradition, each sampler includes a border of floral motifs appropriate for that time of the year, the appropriate zodiac sign and symbol, and a decorative alphabet, with the remainder of the block filled with various decorative motifs. To create your own individual sampler, fill the block with the appropriate motifs taken from any of the other samplers or use other charted designs of your own choice.

The charted design for each sampler is printed over four pages in the book. You may want to remove the necessary pages from the book and tape the entire design together before beginning your work.

Although charted designs can be used in many different forms of needlework, such as needlepoint, latch-hooking, crocheting and knitting, these designs were originally created for counted cross-stitch. Counted cross-stitch is very simple. The basic ingredients are a small, blunt needle and a fabric that is woven so evenly it appears to be formed in regular blocks or squares. Push the threaded needle up through a hole in the fabric and cross over the thread intersection (or square) diagonally, left to right (*diagram 1*). This is half the stitch. Now cross back, right to left, making an X.

DIAGRAM 1

Counted cross-stitch is an ancient skill that has been practiced and perfected with slight variations in technique all over the world. Here in America and in the Scandinavian countries, the bottom stitches traditionally slant left to right and the top stitches right to left. In England, however, the stitches slant in the opposite directions. It really makes no difference which technique you adopt *as long as you are consistent* throughout your piece of work.

In America an embroidery hoop is used, and the work is done with the stab stitch, in which one comes up through a hole in one journey and then goes down through the next hole in a separate journey. In many other parts of the world, however, cross-stitchers use a continuous sewing-stitch motion, and the work is done without a hoop.

One of the great advantages to counted cross-stitch is that the supplies and equipment required are minimal and inexpensive. You will need:

1. A small blunt tapestry needle, #24 or #26.

2. Evenweave fabric. This can be linen, cotton, wool or a blend that includes miracle fabrics. The three most popular fabrics are:

Cotton Aida. This is made 14 threads per inch, 11 threads per inch, 8 threads per inch, and so forth. Fourteen, being the prettiest, is preferred.

Evenweave Linen. This also comes in a variety of threads per inch. Working on evenweave linen involves a slightly different technique, which is explained on page 4. Thirty-count linen will give a stitch approximately the same size as 14-count aida.

Hardanger Cloth. This has 22 threads per inch and is available in cotton or linen.

3. Embroidery thread. This can be six-strand mercerized cotton floss (DMC, Coats and Clark, Lily, Anchor, etc.), crewel wool, Danish Flower Thread, silken and metal threads or perle cotton. DMC embroidery thread has been used to color-code the patterns in this book. For 14-count aida and 30-count linen, divide six-strand cotton floss and work with only two strands. For more texture use more thread. Crewel wool is pretty on an evenweave wool fabric. Danish Flower Thread is a thicker thread with a matt finish, one strand equalling two of cotton floss.

4. Embroidery hoop. Use a plastic or wooden 4", 5" or 6" round or oval hoop with a screw type tension adjuster.

5. A pair of sharp embroidery scissors is absolutely essential.

Prepare the fabric by whipping, hemming, or zigzagging on the sewing machine to prevent ravelling at the edges. Next, locate the exact center of the design you have chosen, so that you can then center the design on the piece of fabric. The designs in the book have an arrow at the top and along one side; follow the indicated rows to where they intersect; this is the center stitch. Next, find the center of the fabric by folding it in half both vertically and horizontally. The center stitch of the design should fall where the creases in the fabric meet.

It's usually not very convenient to begin work with the center stitch itself. As a rule, it's better to start at the top of a design working horizontal rows of a single color, left to right. This technique permits you to go from an unoccupied space to an occupied space (from an empty hole to a filled one), which makes ruffling the floss less likely. To find out where the top of the design should be placed, count squares up from the center of the design, and then count off the corresponding number of holes up from the center of the fabric.

Next, place the section of the fabric to be worked tautly in the hoop; the tighter the better, for tension makes it easier to push the needle through the holes without piercing the fabric. As you work, use the screw adjuster to tighten as necessary. Keep the screw at the top and out of your way. When beginning, fasten the thread with a waste knot by holding a bit of thread on the underside of the work and anchoring it with the first few stitches (*diagram 2*). Do all the stitches in the same color in the same row, working left to right and slanting from bottom left to upper right (*diagram 3*). Then cross back, completing the X's (*diagram 4*). Some cross-stitchers prefer to cross each stitch as they

DIAGRAM 4

DIAGRAM 5

come to it; this is fine, but be sure the slant is always in the correct direction. Of course, isolated stitches must be crossed as you work them. Vertical stitches are crossed as shown in diagram 5. Holes are used more than once; all stitches "hold hands" unless a space is indicated. The work is always held upright, never turned as for some needle-point stitches.

When carrying a color from one area to another, wiggle your needle under existing stitches on the underside. Do not carry a color across an open expanse of fabric for more than a few stitches as the thread will be visible from the front. Remember, in counted cross-stitch you do not work the background.

To end a color, weave in and out of the underside of the stitches, perhaps making a scallop stitch or two for extra security (*diagram 6*). Whenever possible end in the direction in which you are traveling, jumping up a row, if necessary (*diagram 7*). This prevents holes caused by work being pulled in two directions. Do not make knots; knots make bumps. Cut off the ends of the threads; do not leave any tails because they'll show through when the work is mounted.

The only other stitch used in counted cross-stitch is the backstitch. This is worked from hole to hole and may be vertical, horizontal or slanted (*diagram 8*).

Working on linen requires a slightly different technique. Evenweave linen is remarkably regular, but there are always some thin threads and some that are nubbier or fatter than others. To even these out and to make a stitch that is easy to see, the cross-stitch is worked over two threads each way. The "square" you are covering is thus four threads (*diagram 9*). The first few stitches on linen are sometimes difficult, but one quickly begins "to see in twos." After the third stitch, a pattern is established, and should you inadvertently cross over three threads instead of four, the difference in slant will make it immediately apparent that you have erred.

Linen evenweave fabric should be worked with the selvage at the side, not at the top and bottom.

Because you go over more threads, linen affords more var-

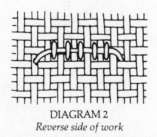

DIAGRAM 2
Reverse side of work

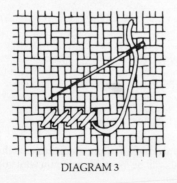

DIAGRAM 3

DIAGRAM 6
Reverse side of work

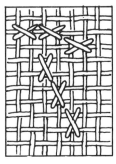

DIAGRAM 10

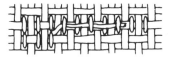

DIAGRAM 7
Reverse side of work

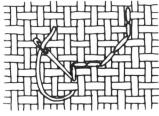

DIAGRAM 8

DIAGRAM 11

DIAGRAM 12

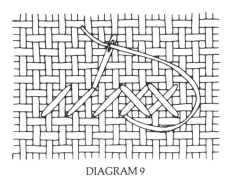

DIAGRAM 9

DIAGRAM 13

iations in stitches. A half cross-stitch can slant in either direction. Diagram 10 shows half cross-stitches worked over one thread in the one direction. A three-quarter cross-stitch is shown in diagram 11. Diagram 12 shows backstitch on linen. Diagram 13 shows four backstitches worked over a single thread and a single thread crossing. A number of the charts in this book were designed specifically for work on linen and call for the use of half cross-stitches and three-quarter cross-stitches. These stitches will have to be worked *between* holes, rather than from hole to hole, when adapted for Aida or Hardanger cloth.

Bear in mind that the finished piece of needlework will not be the same size as the charted design unless you happen to be working on fabric that has the same number of threads per inch as the chart has squares per inch. To determine how large a finished design will be, divide the number of stitches in the design by the thread-count of the fabric. For example, if a design that is 112 stitches wide by 140 stitches deep is worked on a 14-count cloth, divide 112 stitches by 14 to get 8 and 140 by 14 to get 10; so the worked design will measure 8" x 10". The same design worked on 22-count fabric would measure approximately 5" x 6½".

After you have completed your embroidery, wash it in cool or lukewarm water with a mild soap. Rinse well. Do not wring. Roll in a towel to remove excess moisture. Immediately iron on a padded surface with the embroidery face down. Be sure the embroidery is completely dry before attempting to mount.

To mount as a picture, center the embroidery over a pure white, rag-content mat board. Turn margins over to the back evenly. Lace the margins with button thread, top to bottom, side to side. The fabric should be tight and even, with a little tension. Never use glue for mounting. Counted cross-stitch on cotton or linen may be framed under glass. Wool needs to breathe and should not be framed under glass unless breathing space is left.

Your local needlework shop or department where you buy your materials will be happy to help you with any problems.

Aries
The Ram
[TOP]

DMC #

451 Q Dark sea gull grey
451 ···· Dark sea gull grey; *backstitch*
3045 ✕ Dark mustard brown
3045 ✴ Dark mustard brown; *backstitch*
729 ⁄ Medium old gold
3046 ✴ Medium mustard brown
741 ⅄ Orange

725	**V**	Medium saffron gold	368	**U**	Light pistachio green
726	**A**	Light saffron gold	3021	**▲**	Very dark taupe grey
727	**□**	Very light saffron gold	611	**⊞**	Dark drab grey
3078	**—**	Very light golden yellow	612	**Y**	Medium drab grey
3013	**L**	Medium khaki green	3328	**✳**	Medium red morocco
501	**‖**	Blue green	3328	**—**	Medium red morocco; *backstitch*
502	**O**	Dark almond green		**·**	White

Aries
The Ram
[BOTTOM]

DMC #
451 **Q** Dark sea gull grey
451 **····** Dark sea gull grey; *backstitch*
3045 **✕** Dark mustard brown
3045 **╫** Dark mustard brown; *backstitch*
729 **⁄** Medium old gold
3046 **◥** Medium mustard brown
741 **↘** Orange

725 $\textbf{V}$ Medium saffron gold
726 $\textbf{A}$ Light saffron gold
727 $\boxed{}$ Very light saffron gold
3078 — Very light golden yellow
3013 $\textbf{L}$ Medium khaki green
501 $\parallel$ Blue green
502 $\textbf{O}$ Dark almond green

368 $\textbf{U}$ Light pistachio green
3021 $\blacktriangle$ Very dark taupe grey
611 $\boxplus$ Dark drab grey
612 $\textbf{Y}$ Medium drab grey
3328 $\maltese$ Medium red morocco
3328 — Medium red morocco; *backstitch*
• White

Taurus
The Bull
[TOP]

DMC #

451 **Q** Dark sea gull grey
3045 **X** Dark mustard brown
3045 **⋕** Dark mustard brown; *backstitch*
610 **⊞** Very dark drab grey
610 **—** Very dark drab grey; *backstitch*
3346 **✕** Beetle green

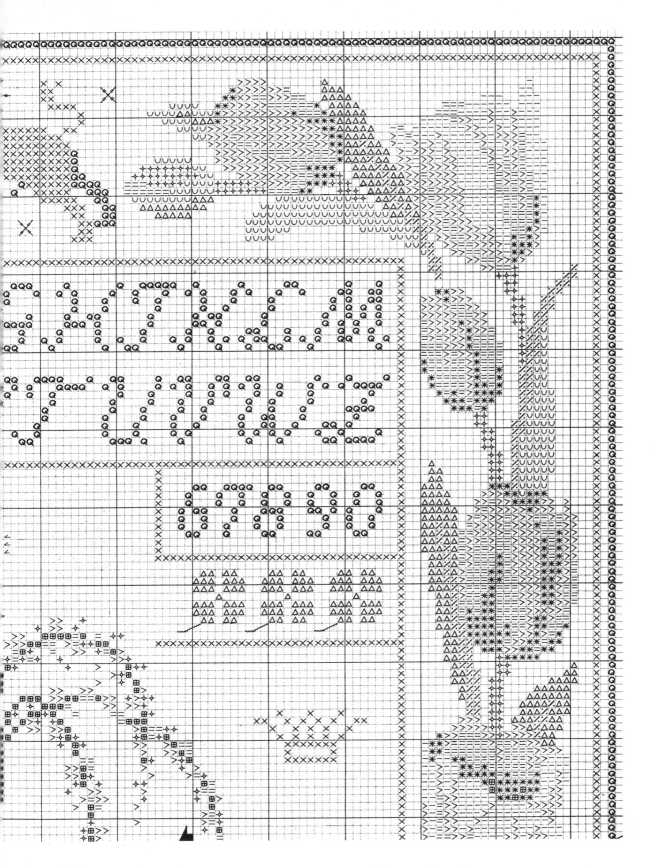

320 △ Medium pistachio green
320 ∿ Medium pistachio green; *backstitch*
368 U Light pistachio green
3348 ✢ Light beetle green
221 ● Ultra dark faded pink
793 ⊟ Medium cornflower blue

794 ∟ Light cornflower blue
602 ✱ Dark cerise
962 ═ Medium old rose
894 > Light geranium pink
776 — Medium pink

Taurus
The Bull
[BOTTOM]

DMC #

- 451 **Q** Dark sea gull grey
- 3045 **X** Dark mustard brown
- 3045 **⧓** Dark mustard brown; *backstitch*
- 610 **⊞** Very dark drab grey
- 610 **—** Very dark drab grey; *backstitch*
- 3346 **✕** Beetle green

320 △ Medium pistachio green
320 〜 Medium pistachio green; *backstitch*
368 ∪ Light pistachio green
3348 ✦ Light beetle green
221 ● Ultra dark faded pink
793 ⊟ Medium cornflower blue

794 ⌐ Light cornflower blue
602 ✳ Dark cerise
962 ＝ Medium old rose
894 ＞ Light geranium pink
776 — Medium pink

Gemini
The Twins
[TOP]

DMC #

936 ● Very dark moss green
581 ℓ Moss green
471 ✕ Very light moss green
472 ✕ Ultra very light moss green
337 ▲ Dark brown
610 ⊞ Very dark drab grey
3045 ✕ Dark mustard brown

210 ↙ Medium parma violet
209 ↑ Dark parma violet
553 ⊙ Medium violet
327 ◆ Dark scabius violet
451 — Dull sea gull grey; *backstitch*
451 Ϙ Dull sea gull grey
3045 # Dark mustard brown; *backstitch*

3688 ÷ Medium raspberry red
3687 ⊘ Dark raspberry red
3685 L Very dark raspberry red
742 ▲ Dark yellow
211 T Light parma violet

Gemini
The Twins
[BOTTOM]

DMC #
936 ● Very dark moss green
581 ♎ Moss green
471 ∴ Very light moss green
472 ◇ Ultra very light moss green
337 ▲ Dark brown
610 ⊞ Very dark drab grey
3045 ✕ Dark mustard brown

3045 ✖ Dark mustard brown; *backstitch*
451 **Q** Dull sea gull grey
451 — Dull sea gull grey; *backstitch*
327 ◆ Dark scabius violet
553 ☉ Medium violet
209 ↓ Dark parma violet
210 ⤺ Medium parma violet

211 **T** Light parma violet
742 **A** Dark yellow
3685 ⊥ Very dark raspberry red
3687 ◖ Dark raspberry red
3688 ⊸ Medium raspberry red

Cancer The Crab
[TOP]

DMC #

3051 ● Dark green
3052 ☒ Dark tawny green
451 ○ Dark sea gull grey
451 ⋯ Dark sea gull grey; backstitch
415 ╱ Silver grey
• White
580 ☐ Dark moss green

470 ℝ Light moss green
471 ⁒ Very light moss green
817 ♥ Ultra dark geranium red
350 ✕ Dark geranium red
351 3 Medium coral
352 ⊙ Medium geranium red
353 = Peach

327 # Dark scabius violet
792 ⊟ Dark cornflower blue
793 ← Medium cornflower blue
3045 ✕ Dark mustard brown
3045 ## Dark mustard brown; *backstitch*

Cancer
The Crab
[BOTTOM]

DMC #

- 3051 ● Dark green
- 3052 ◨ Dark tawny green
- 451 ℚ Dark sea gull grey
- 451 ••• Dark sea gull grey; *backstitch*
- 415 ╱ Silver grey
- • White
- 580 ⊡ Dark moss green

470 ♞ Light moss green
471 ⁄ Very light moss green
817 ♥ Ultra dark geranium red
350 ✕ Dark geranium red
351 3 Medium coral
352 ⊙ Medium geranium red
353 = Peach

327 # Dark scabius violet
792 ⊟ Dark cornflower blue
793 ← Medium cornflower blue
3045 ✕ Dark mustard brown
3045 ＃ Dark mustard brown; *backstitch*

Leo
The Lion
[TOP]

DMC #

610 ⊞ Very dark drab grey
610 — Very dark drab grey; *backstitch*
3045 ✗ Dark mustard brown
3045 ## Dark mustard brown; *backstitch*
451 Q Dark sea gull grey
451 ⋯ Dark sea gull grey; *backstitch*

MICHAEL

8-12-1988

3051 ● Dark green
3052 ◨ Dark tawny brown
3053 ⁄ Medium tawny brown
3013 Y Medium khaki green
471 ♣ Very light moss green
900 ♥ Dark flame orange red

351 ⊙ Medium coral
351 ∿ Medium coral; *backstitch*
352 = Medium geranium red
783 ♪ Topaz
725 6 Medium saffron gold
973 ↘ Very light orange yellow

Leo
The Lion
[BOTTOM]

DMC #

610	⊞	Very dark drab grey
610	—	Very dark drab grey; *backstitch*
3045	✗	Dark mustard brown
3045	#⧣	Dark mustard brown; *backstitch*
451	Q	Dark sea gull grey
451	⋯	Dark sea gull grey; *backstitch*

3051 ● Dark green
3052 ◪ Dark tawny brown
3053 ╱ Medium tawny brown
3013 Y Medium khaki green
471 ℛ Very light moss green
900 ♥ Dark flame orange red

351 ☉ Medium coral
351 ∾ Medium coral; *backstitch*
352 ═ Medium geranium red
783 ℘ Topaz
725 6 Medium saffron gold
973 ↘ Very light orange yellow

Virgo
The Virgin
[TOP]

DMC #

580	●	Dark moss green
470	∷	Light moss green
471	△	Very light moss green
472	+	Ultra very light moss green
552	◢	Dark violet
553	⊙	Medium violet
554	1	Light violet

725 **A** Medium saffron gold
726 **P** Light saffron gold
611 **⊞** Dark drab grey
420 **6** Dark hazel nut brown
3045 **L** Dark mustard brown
3045 **⊬** Dark mustard brown; *backstitch*
844 **■** Ultra dark beaver grey

844 **〰** Ultra dark beaver grey; *backstitch*
451 **↓** Dark sea gull grey
451 **⋯** Dark sea gull grey; *backstitch*
3024 **✳** Very light taupe grey
312 **⊤** Light navy blue
312 **—** Light navy blue; *backstitch*
309 **✳** Deep rose

Virgo
The Virgin
[BOTTOM]

DMC #		
580	●	Dark moss green
470	∷	Light moss green
471	△	Very light moss green
472	+	Ultra very light moss green
552	/	Dark violet
553	⊙	Medium violet
554	1	Light violet

[BOTTOM]

725 A Medium saffron gold
726 P Light saffron gold
611 ⊞ Dark drab grey
420 6 Dark hazel nut brown
3045 L Dark mustard brown
3045 + Dark mustard brown; backstitch
844 ■ Ultra dark beaver grey

844 ⟋⟍ Ultra dark beaver grey; backstitch
451 ↑ Dark sea gull grey
451 ⋯ Dark sea gull grey; backstitch
3024 ✳ Very light taupe grey
312 ⌐ Light navy blue
312 — Light navy blue; backstitch
309 ✳ Deep rose

Libra
The Balance
[TOP]

DMC #

400	➘	Dark mahogany
900	⊙	Dark flame orange red
947	K	Light fire red
733	Q	Medium yellow green
734	X	Light yellow green
831	●	Dark olive green
833	↗	Light olive green
676	⑀	Light old gold

3045 L Dark mustard brown
3045 ◣ Dark mustard brown; 3/4 stitch
3045 ↕ Dark mustard brown; *backstitch*
783 A Topaz
451 ↓ Dark sea gull grey
451 ↓ Dark sea gull grey; *backstitch*
415 Z Silver grey
610 ▲ Very dark drab grey

610 ⋮ Very dark drab grey; *backstitch*
792 ⊟ Dark cornflower blue
792 | Dark cornflower blue; *backstitch*
598 ← Light greenish grey
3346 ‖ Beetle green
922 ✕ Light rust brown
922 ⌇ Light rust brown; *backstitch*
⁄·⁄ White; *3/4 stitch*

Libra
The Balance
[BOTTOM]

DMC #

400	◣	Dark mahogany
900	⊙	Dark flame orange red
947	K	Light fire red
733	Q	Medium yellow green
734	X	Light yellow green
831	●	Dark olive green
833	✗	Light olive green
676	◤	Light old gold

3045 └ Dark mustard brown

3045 ⩍ Dark mustard brown; *¾ stitch*

3045 ⇕ Dark mustard brown; *backstitch*

783 A Topaz

451 ↓ Dark sea gull grey

451 ↯ Dark sea gull grey; *backstitch*

415 z Silver grey

610 ▲ Very dark drab grey

610 ⦂ Very dark drab grey; *backstitch*

792 ⊟ Dark cornflower blue

792 I Dark cornflower blue; *backstitch*

598 ⬸ Light greenish grey

3346 ‖ Beetle green

922 ✕ Light rust brown

922 ⨍ Light rust brown; *backstitch*

/· ⟍ White; *¾ stitch*

Scorpio
The Scorpion
[TOP]

DMC #

311	◆	Medium navy blue
930	✕	Dark antique blue
221	◤	Ultra dark faded blue
356	✕	Medium terra cotta
610	⊞	Very dark drab grey

420 **6** Dark hazel nut brown

3045 **X** Dark mustard brown

3045 **✗** Dark mustard brown; *backstitch*

676 **T** Light old gold

433 **▲** Medium brown

435 **Φ** Golden brown

451 **Q** Dark sea gull grey

3012 **∷** Dark khaki green

3012 **/** Dark khaki green; *backstitch*

Scorpio
The Scorpion
[BOTTOM]

DMC #

311 ◆ Medium navy blue
930 ✕ Dark antique blue
221 ◢ Ultra dark faded blue
356 ✕ Medium terra cotta
610 ⊞ Very dark drab grey

420 **6** Dark hazel nut brown

3045 **X** Dark mustard brown

3045 **✗** Dark mustard brown; *backstitch*

676 **T** Light old gold

433 **▲** Medium brown

435 **Φ** Golden brown

451 **Q** Dark sea gull grey

3012 **∷** Dark khaki green

3012 **╱** Dark khaki green; *backstitch*

Sagittarius
The Archer
[TOP]

DMC #
349 ♥ Very dark geranium red
351 ≡ Medium coral
420 6 Dark hazel nut brown
3045 ✕ Dark mustard brown
3045 ✚ Dark mustard brown; *backstitch*
833 ☐ Light olive green
3023 ✔ Light taupe grey

3024 ⠂ Very light taupe grey

895 ● Ultra dark scarab green

3346 ╱ Beetle green

3347 ∪ Medium beetle green

310 ■ Black

451 Q Dark sea gull grey

451 — Dark sea gull grey; *backstitch*

501 ‖ Blue green

502 𝑂 Dark almond green

927 L Medium grey green

921 ✗ Medium henna brown

922 ⊂ Light rust brown

839 ⊞ Dark beige brown

Sagittarius
The Archer
[BOTTOM]

DMC #

349 ♥ Very dark geranium red
351 ≋ Medium coral
420 6 Dark hazel nut brown
3045 ✕ Dark mustard brown
3045 ✛ Dark mustard brown; *backstitch*
833 ▢ Light olive green
3023 ↓ Light taupe grey

3024 .° Very light taupe grey

895 ● Ultra dark scarab green

3346 ╱ Beetle green

3347 U Medium beetle green

310 ■ Black

451 Q Dark sea gull grey

451 — Dark sea gull grey; *backstitch*

501 II Blue green

502 ∅ Dark almond green

927 L Medium grey green

921 ✕ Medium henna brown

922 C Light rust brown

839 ⊞ Dark beige brown

Capricorn
The Goat
[TOP]

DMC #

315 ⊥ Ultra dark mauve	223 ◇ Dark faded pink
315 — Ultra dark mauve; *backstitch*	3354 ⊓ Light old rose
3350 ◖ Very dark old rose	778 T Medium mauve
3350 •• Very dark old rose; *backstitch*	580 ∴ Dark moss green
3350 ⊟ Very dark old rose; *half cross-stitch*	471 Ⴍ Very light moss green
	844 ■ Ultra dark beaver grey
	844 ⋯ Ultra dark beaver grey; *backstitch*

844 🞐 Ultra dark beaver grey;
    half cross-stitch

415 ✳ Silver grey

762 **Z** Very light ash grey

451 **Q** Dark sea gull grey

451 ⌣ Dark sea gull grey;
    backstitch

451 🞑 Dark sea gull grey;
    half cross-stitch

3052 • Dark tawny brown

3053 **Ø** Medium tawny brown

312 ⊟ Light navy blue

312 ⧾⧾Light navy blue; *backstitch*

3012 ♠ Dark khaki green

3013 ⊡ Medium khaki green

611 ⊞ Dark drab grey

611 ◄◄Dark drab grey; *backstitch*

3045 **6** Dark mustard brown

3045 ∞ Dark mustard brown;
    backstitch

3045 🞓 Dark mustard brown;
    half cross-stitch

677 **Y** Very light old gold

677 ⊟ Very light old gold;
    half cross-stitch

Capricorn
The Goat
[BOTTOM]

DMC #

315 ⊥ Ultra dark mauve
315 — Ultra dark mauve;
backstitch
3350 ◗ Very dark old rose
3350 •• Very dark old rose;
backstitch
3350 ⊟ Very dark old rose;
half cross-stitch

223 ◈ Dark faded pink
3354 ⊓ Light old rose
778 T Medium mauve
580 ∴ Dark moss green
471 ♀ Very light moss green
844 ■ Ultra dark beaver grey
844 ••• Ultra dark beaver grey;
backstitch

844 ▫ Ultra dark beaver grey;
    half cross-stitch
415 ✗ Silver grey
762 Z Very light ash grey
451 Q Dark sea gull grey
451 ∿ Dark sea gull grey;
    backstitch
451 ▫ Dark sea gull grey;
    half cross-stitch

3052 ˙. Dark tawny brown
3053 Ø Medium tawny brown
312 ⊟ Light navy blue
312 ╫ Light navy blue; *backstitch*
3012 ♠ Dark khaki green
3013 ⊡ Medium khaki green
611 ⊞ Dark drab grey
611 ◄◄ Dark drab grey; *backstitch*
3045 6 Dark mustard brown

3045 ∞ Dark mustard brown;
    backstitch
3045 ▣ Dark mustard brown;
    half cross-stitch
677 Y Very light old gold
677 ▣ Very light old gold;
    half cross-stitch

Aquarius
The Water Bearer
[TOP]

DMC #
3345 ♥ Very dark beetle green
469 Q Moss green
471 U Very light moss green
471 ⋯ Very light moss green; *backstitch*
972 A Light orange yellow
444 T Medium buttercup
307 ⋎ Medium lemon yellow

734 ▮▮ Light yellow green
793 ◡ Medium cornflower blue
792 ⊟ Dark cornflower blue
• White
844 ◼ Ultra dark beaver grey
451 ▼ Dark sea gull grey
451 — Dark sea gull grey; *backstitch*

3045 ϭ Dark mustard brown
832 ◣ Medium olive green
832 ╫ Medium olive green; *backstitch*
3328 ✳ Medium red morocco
3328 〰 Medium red morocco; *backstitch*

Aquarius
The Water Bearer
[BOTTOM]

DMC #

3345	♥	Very dark beetle green
469	Q	Moss green
471	U	Very light moss green
471	⋯	Very light moss green; *backstitch*
972	A	Light orange yellow
444	T	Medium buttercup
307	⅄	Medium lemon yellow

734 ▮▮ Light yellow green
793 ↙ Medium cornflower blue
792 ⊟ Dark cornflower blue
• White
844 ◼ Ultra dark beaver grey
451 ▼ Dark sea gull grey
451 — Dark sea gull grey; *backstitch*

3045 6 Dark mustard brown
832 ◣ Medium olive green
832 ⊞⊞ Medium olive green; *backstitch*
3328 ✳ Medium red morocco
3328 〰 Medium red morocco; *backstitch*

49

Pisces
The Fishes
[TOP]

DMC #

3345 ● Dark mustard brown
320 ╱ Medium pistachio green
320 ◄◄ Medium pistachio green; *backstitch*
369 ∪ Very light pistachio green
741 ↘ Orange
327 ⊞ Dark scabius violet
553 ⊙ Medium violet
211 N Light parma violet

210 T Medium parma violet
3045 X Dark mustard brown
3045 ╫ Dark mustard brown; *backstitch*
451 Q Dark sea gull grey
451 ⋯ Dark sea gull grey; *backstitch*
844 ■ Ultra dark beaver grey
844 — Ultra dark beaver grey; *backstitch*
645 Y Very dark beaver grey

647 ✖ Medium beaver grey
648 Z Light beaver grey
3350 ● Very dark old rose
3354 > Light old rose
433 ▲ Medium brown
435 ◑ Golden brown
712 ∴ Very dark cream

Pisces
The Fishes
[BOTTOM]

DMC #

- 3345 ● Dark mustard brown
- 320 ⁄ Medium pistachio green
- 320 ↤ Medium pistachio green; *backstitch*
- 369 U Very light pistachio green
- 741 ↘ Orange
- 327 ⊞ Dark scabius violet
- 553 ☉ Medium violet
- 211 N Light parma violet

210 T Medium parma violet
3045 X Dark mustard brown
3045 ⊞ Dark mustard brown; *backstitch*
451 Q Dark sea gull grey
451 ⋯ Dark sea gull grey; *backstitch*
844 ▪ Ultra dark beaver grey
844 — Ultra dark beaver grey; *backstitch*
645 Y Very dark beaver grey

647 ✳ Medium beaver grey
648 Z Light beaver grey
3350 ⊖ Very dark old rose
3354 > Light old rose
433 ▲ Medium brown
435 ① Golden brown
712 .· Very dark cream

DOVER BOOKS ON NEEDLEPOINT, EMBROIDERY

BASIC NEEDLERY STITCHES ON MESH FABRICS, Mary Ann Beinecke. (21713-2) $3.00

DESIGNS AND PATTERNS FOR EMBROIDERERS AND CRAFTSMEN, Wm. Briggs and Company Ltd. (23030-9) $4.50

HARDANGER EMBROIDERY, Sigrid Bright. (23592-0) $1.50

FRUIT AND VEGETABLE IRON-ON TRANSFER PATTERNS, Barbara Christopher. (23556-4) $1.50

NEEDLEWORK ALPHABETS AND DESIGNS, Blanche Cirker (ed.). (23159-3) $2.25

AMERICAN INDIAN NEEDLEPOINT DESIGNS, Roslyn Epstein. (22973-4) $1.50

DANISH PULLED THREAD EMBROIDERY, Esther Fangel, Ida Winckler and Agnete Madsen. (23474-6) $3.00

PATCHWORK QUILT DESIGNS FOR NEEDLEPOINT, Frank Fontana. (23300-6) $1.50

CHARTED FOLK DESIGNS FOR CROSS-STITCH EMBROIDERY, Maria Foris and Andreas Foris. (23191-7) $2.95

BLACKWORK EMBROIDERY, Elisabeth Geddes and Moyra McNeill. (23245-X) $3.50

VICTORIAN ALPHABETS, MONOGRAMS AND NAMES FOR NEEDLEWORKERS, Godey's Lady's Book. (23072-4) $3.50

VICTORIAN NEEDLEPOINT DESIGNS, Godey's Lady's Book and Peterson's Magazine. (23163-1) $1.75

A TREASURY OF CHARTED DESIGNS FOR NEEDLEWORKERS, Georgia L. Gorham and Jeanne M. Warth. (23558-0) $1.50

GEOMETRIC NEEDLEPOINT DESIGNS, Carol Belanger Grafton. (23160-7) $1.75

FULL-COLOR BICENTENNIAL NEEDLEPOINT DESIGNS, Carol Belanger Grafton. (23233-6) $2.00

FULL-COLOR RUSSIAN FOLK NEEDLEPOINT DESIGNS, Frieda Halpern. (23451-7) $2.25

WHITE WORK: TECHNIQUES AND DESIGNS, Carter Houck (ed.). (23695-1) $1.75

CLASSIC POSTERS FOR NEEDLEPOINT, M. Elizabeth Irvine. (23640-4) $1.50

FAVORITE PETS IN CHARTED DESIGNS, Barbara Johansson. (23889-X) $1.75

CREATIVE STITCHES, Edith John. (22972-6) $3.50

NEW STITCHES FOR NEEDLECRAFT, Edith John. (22971-8) $3.00

PERSIAN RUG MOTIFS FOR NEEDLEPOINT, Lyatif Kerimov. (23187-9) $2.00

CHARTED PEASANT DESIGNS FROM SAXON TRANSYLVANIA, Heinz Kiewe. (23425-8) $2.00

Paperbound unless otherwise indicated. Prices subject to change without notice. Available at your book dealer or write for free catalogues to Dept. Needlework, Dover Publications, Inc., 180 Varick Street, New York, N.Y. 10014. Please indicate field of interest. Each year Dover publishes over 200 books on fine art, music, crafts and needlework, antiques, languages, literature, children's books, chess, cookery, nature, anthropology, science, mathematics, and other areas.

Manufactured in the U.S.A.